NATIONAL GEOGRAPHIC

Ladders

ONWARD!

Bottom of the World

by Michael Bilski

There is a place that gets very little **precipitation** in a year. It gets hardly any drizzle, rain, snow, or sleet. The **temperature** can drop to –94°F (–70°C). The mountains are icy. The land is frozen. This is the **continent** of Antarctica at the bottom of the world. The **South Pole** is a place in Antarctica.

Haiku 1

Bottom of the world

Continent like no other

Stark Antarctica!

Haiku 2

World's coldest desert

Freezing in the ice and wind

Is it ever warm?

Haiku 3

Lure to explorers

Brave men who would not give up

Onward to the Pole!

The Heroic Age of Antarctic Exploration

by Michael Bilski

In the early 1900s, Antarctica was a new place to explore. Brave men from around the world explored the **continent.** They faced cold and stormy weather. But the men pressed **onward.** Roald Amundsen, Robert Falcon Scott, and Ernest Shackleton were three of the explorers.

Antarctic Explorers

Erich von Drygalski
German South Polar
Expedition, 1901–1903

Roald Amundsen
Norwegian Antarctic
Expedition, 1910–1912

*First to reach South Pole
(December 14, 1911)*

Adriene de Gerlache
Belgian Antarctic
Expedition, 1897–1899

William Speirs Bruce
Scottish National
Antarctic Expedition,
1902–1904

Ernest Shackleton
British Antarctic
Expedition, 1907–1909

Imperial Trans-Antarctic
Expedition, 1914–1917

Shackleton-Rowett
Expedition, 1921–1922

Carsten Borchgrevink
British Antarctic
Expedition, 1898–1900

Jean-Baptiste Charcot
French Antarctic
Expedition, 1903–1905
and 1908–1910

Nobu Shirase
Japanese Antarctic
Expedition, 1910–1912

Nils Otto Nordenskjold
Swedish South Polar
Expedition, 1901–1903

Robert Falcon Scott
British National Antarctic
Expedition, 1901–1904

British Antarctic
Expedition, 1910–1913

*Reached South Pole
(January 17, 1912)*

Douglas Mawson
Australasian Antarctic
Expedition, 1911–1914

Rival Explorers

Roald Amundsen

Roald Amundsen was born in Norway. He explored the Arctic. He learned to survive in cold weather. He wore reindeer clothing. He learned about using sled dogs. Amundsen wanted to be the first to reach the **North Pole.** But other men reached the North Pole first. So Amundsen decided that he would be the first to reach the **South Pole.** Robert Scott had the same goal. The race was on!

Robert Falcon Scott

Robert Falcon Scott was born in England. He was in the navy. Scott brought a team on his first **expedition** to Antarctica. They came within 400 miles of the South Pole. Scott wanted to lead the first expedition to reach the South Pole. So he went back to Antarctica. Amundsen had the same goal. But Scott would not give up.

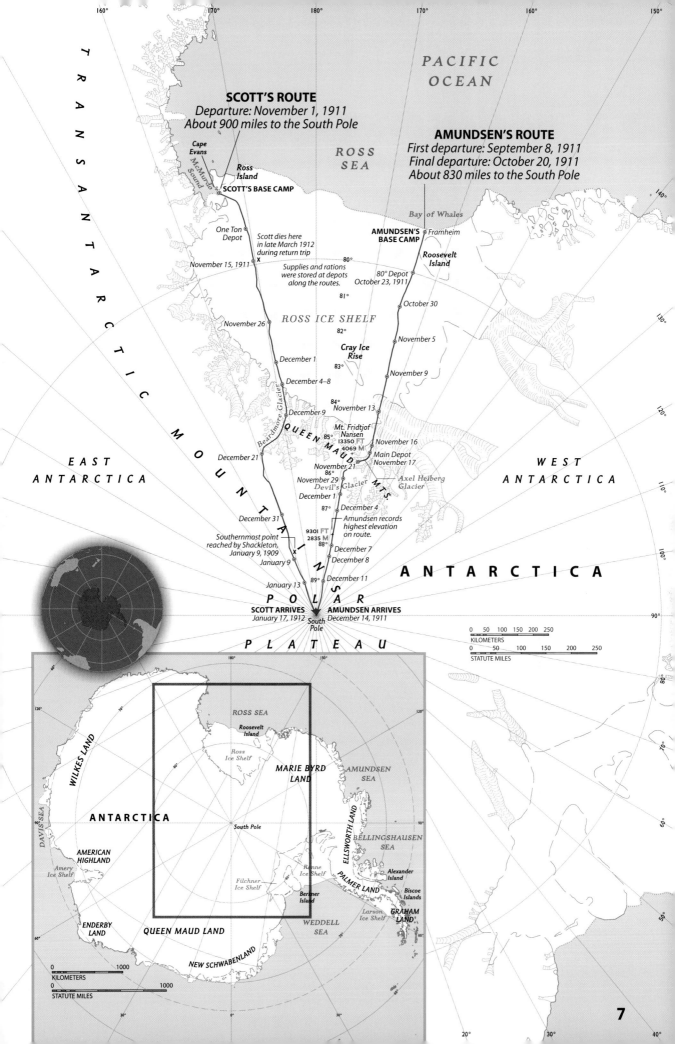

SCOTT'S ROUTE
Departure: November 1, 1911
About 900 miles to the South Pole

AMUNDSEN'S ROUTE
First departure: September 8, 1911
Final departure: October 20, 1911
About 830 miles to the South Pole

PACIFIC
OCEAN

ROSS
SEA

*Cape
Evans*

*Ross
Island*

SCOTT'S BASE CAMP

McMurdo Sound

Bay of Whales

**AMUNDSEN'S
BASE CAMP** • *Framheim*

T
R
A
N
S
A
N
T
A
R
C
T
I
C

*One Ton
Depot*

*Scott dies here
in late March 1912
during return trip*

November 15, 1911 x

80°

*Supplies and rations
were stored at depots
along the routes.*

*Roosevelt
Island*

80° Depot
October 23, 1911

81°

October 30

ROSS ICE SHELF

82°

November 5

*Cray Ice
Rise*

83°

November 9

November 26

December 1

December 4–8

84°
November 13

December 9

85°
*Mt. Fridtjof
Nansen*
13350 FT
4069 M

November 16

Beardmore Glacier

QUEEN MAUD

December 21

Main Depot
November 17

86°
November 21

M
O
U
N
T
A
I
N
S

November 29
Devil's Glacier
December 1

*Axel Heiberg
Glacier*

MTS.

87°
December 4

EAST
ANTARCTICA

December 31

9301 FT
2835 M

*Amundsen records
highest elevation
on route.*

WEST
ANTARCTICA

*Southernmost point
reached by Shackleton,
January 9, 1909*
January 9

88°

December 7

December 8

ANTARCTICA

January 13

89°

December 11

P O L A R

SCOTT ARRIVES
January 17, 1912

AMUNDSEN ARRIVES
December 14, 1911

*South
Pole*

P L A T E A U

0 50 100 150 200 250
KILOMETERS
0   50   100   150   200   250
STATUTE MILES

ROSS SEA

*Roosevelt
Island*

*Ross
Ice Shelf*

MARIE BYRD
LAND

AMUNDSEN
SEA

WILKES LAND

ANTARCTICA

South Pole

BELLINGSHAUSEN
SEA

DAVIS SEA

AMERICAN
HIGHLAND

ELLSWORTH LAND

*Alexander
Island*

*Amery
Ice Shelf*

*Ronne
Ice Shelf*

PALMER
LAND

*Biscoe
Islands*

ENDERBY
LAND

*Filchner
Ice Shelf*

*Berkner
Island*

WEDDELL
SEA

*Larsen
Ice Shelf*

GRAHAM
LAND

QUEEN MAUD LAND

NEW SCHWABENLAND

0   1000
KILOMETERS
0   1000
STATUTE MILES

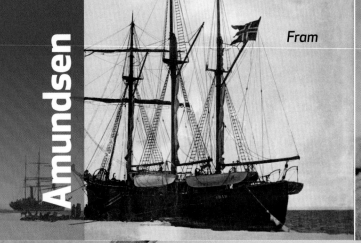

Fram

Amundsen

Amundsen

The Pole Is the Goal

Amundsen and Scott each wanted to reach the South Pole first. Who would win the race?

Scott and his **crew** sailed in their ship, *Terra Nova*. They arrived in Antarctica in January 1911. They brought dogs, ponies, and sleds. Scott and his men set up **depots** on the way to the South Pole. They stored food and supplies in the depots. But one of their sleds broke. The ponies struggled in the cold. They could not get their biggest depot as close to the Pole as they wanted to.

Terra Nova

Scott

Scott

Sled at a supply depot

Amundsen and his crew sailed in their ship, *Fram*. They arrived in Antarctica 11 days after Scott. They set up camp. It took them nine months to get ready for their trip to the South Pole.

Amundsen remembered what he had learned in the Arctic. He brought almost 100 sled dogs. He also brought food, supplies, and fresh water. Amundsen and his crew waited for the warmer weather in spring. They trained the dogs. They practiced skiing. They set up depots along the way to the South Pole. The men used the sleds and dogs to get their depots close to the Pole. Amundsen's crew ate well and slept well for the trip ahead.

Dog team

Amundsen's team at the South Pole

Testing the sea's depth with a hammer

Victory and Defeat

Amundsen and his crew left for the South Pole in October. They took four sleds and more than 50 dogs. The food depots did the trick. The men skied and the dogs pulled the sleds. They climbed mountains. They battled storms. But the crew pressed onward. They finally reached the Pole in December. There was no sign of Scott. Amundsen and his men had won the race! They planted a flag and set up a tent.

Scott and his crew left for the South Pole in November. They took 10 ponies, sleds, and more than 20 dogs. But some of the sleds broke. The ponies couldn't make it through the ice and snow. A storm stopped them for four days.

Both explorers chose their teams and equipment differently.

AMUNDSEN'S TEAM ■ Survived trip ☐ Did not survive

SCOTT'S TEAM

As planned, these men turned back before reaching the South Pole.

The total number of sleds is uncertain. Two were brought back by returning men.

Scott

Crossing a glacier on foot

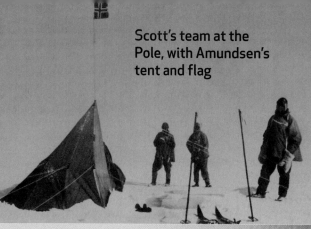

Scott's team at the Pole, with Amundsen's tent and flag

Scott's team had to continue on foot. They were not good skiers. Plus they had to pull their own sleds. So Scott sent most of his crew back to camp. He took four men with him to the South Pole. They saw Amundsen's tent and flag in the distance. They knew they had lost the race. Scott and his men reached the South Pole the next day. They found supplies that Amundsen had left for them.

Amundsen's team had made it back safely. Scott's team did not. They were hungry, sick, and tired. The men were trapped by a storm. They were just 11 miles from their main depot. They never made it there. Scott's diary entry ended the story.

"We shall stick it out to the end, but we are getting weaker, of course, and the end cannot be far. It seems a pity, but I do not think I can write more."

All surviving dogs were brought back by returning team members.

Shackleton's Endurance

Sled dogs watch *Endurance* sink.

Ernest Henry Shackleton

Ernest Henry Shackleton was born in Ireland. He was part of Scott's crew. He was with Scott on his first trip to the South Pole. Shackleton led his own expedition after that. He set a record. He got closer to the South Pole than anyone had before that time.

Amundsen was the first to reach the South Pole. But Shackleton wanted to explore Antarctica on foot. His expedition planned to start at the Weddell Sea. He would then

This map traces their route.

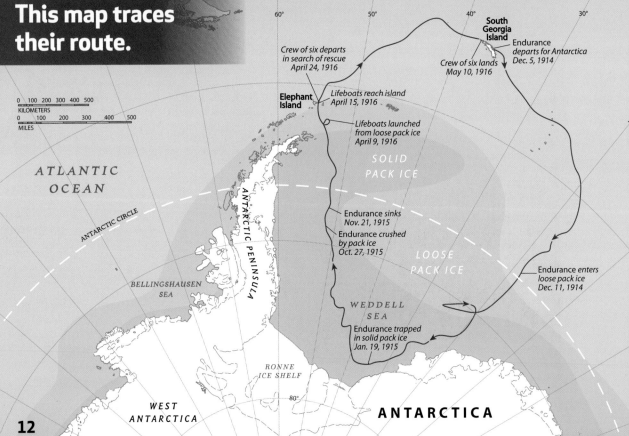

Crew of six departs in search of rescue April 24, 1916

South Georgia Island

Endurance departs for Antarctica Dec. 5, 1914

Crew of six lands May 10, 1916

Elephant Island

Lifeboats reach island April 15, 1916

Lifeboats launched from loose pack ice April 9, 1916

SOLID PACK ICE

ATLANTIC OCEAN

ANTARCTIC CIRCLE

ANTARCTIC PENINSULA

Endurance sinks Nov. 21, 1915

Endurance crushed by pack ice Oct. 27, 1915

LOOSE PACK ICE

Endurance enters loose pack ice Dec. 11, 1914

BELLINGSHAUSEN SEA

WEDDELL SEA

Endurance trapped in solid pack ice Jan. 19, 1915

RONNE ICE SHELF

WEST ANTARCTICA

ANTARCTICA

cross a part of Antarctica that had never been explored. Then he planned to head to the Pole and to the Ross Sea.

Shackleton sailed in his ship, *Endurance*. The ship became trapped in drifting ice. It was trapped for ten long months. They never reached Antarctica. The expedition was doomed. Shackleton and his men stored supplies on *Endurance*. But the ice was slowly crushing the ship. So the men removed their supplies and lifeboats. *Endurance* was crushed and later sank.

Shackleton and his crew drifted on the ice for five more months. It was very cold. They ate whale and seal meat. They were finally able to escape the ice. They sailed their lifeboats to Elephant Island.

Shackleton and his men were trapped on the ice. They didn't set foot on land for more than a year.

Shackleton knew the only hope for rescue was to find a larger ship. Shackleton and a crew of five men sailed a lifeboat 800 miles to South Georgia Island. It was a dangerous mission. They found a ship that could bring them back to rescue the rest of the crew. It took many tries. But every member of Shackleton's expedition was rescued. The men had been away for more than two years. The expedition was a failure. But the story had a heroic end. Shackleton and his crew had endured.

Shackleton reunited with some members of the *Endurance* crew five years later. They planned to sail a new ship, *Quest*. They hoped to sail around Antarctica. Shackleton had a heart attack while on the ship. He was buried on South Georgia Island.

Shackleton's crew on board *Quest*

End of the Heroic Age

This heroic age ended when Shackleton died. The final continent had been explored. Both Amundsen and Scott had reached the South Pole. But people continue to explore Antarctica. Today's explorers are scientists. They come from all over the world to study this frozen land.

Endurance

Check In | What did Scott, Amundsen, and Shackleton have in common? How were they different?

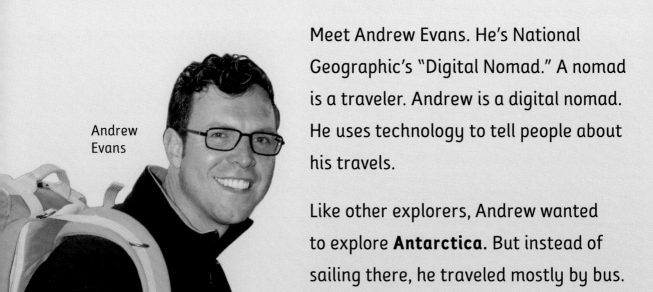

Andrew Evans

Meet Andrew Evans. He's National Geographic's "Digital Nomad." A nomad is a traveler. Andrew is a digital nomad. He uses technology to tell people about his travels.

Like other explorers, Andrew wanted to explore **Antarctica**. But instead of sailing there, he traveled mostly by bus. People followed Andrew's journey on his **blog**. He posted news every day.

Andrew's Antarctic Adventure

by Michael Bilski

Tools

The explorers Amundsen, Scott, and Shackleton used tools to navigate. A compass and a sextant helped them find their way toward the **South Pole**. They recorded their trip using large box cameras.

Explorers today have tools that use GPS. This stands for "Global Positioning System." GPS receivers, digital cameras, and the Internet help explorers find their way. The tools also help them record their journeys. Andrew always takes small cameras with him.

Present	Past
 *Cell-phone compass*	 *Compass*
 *GPS receiver*	 *Sextant*
 *Waterproof camera*	 *Box camera*

Heading South

Andrew got on the bus. He left from the National Geographic offices in Washington, DC. Before he left, Andrew had asked blog readers to help him pick songs. The songs helped pass the time on the long bus ride.

ATLANTIC OCEAN

Andrew visited Cartagena, Colombia. Cartagena has narrow streets. It has old Spanish buildings. Every house, door, and shutter is a different color.

UNITED STATES

MEXICO

BELIZE

GUATEMALA

HONDURAS

EL SALVADOR

NICARAGUA

COSTA RICA

PANAMA

VENEZUELA

COLOMBIA

ECUADOR

PERU

In Costa Rica, Andrew saw streams from his bus window. He also saw macaws, toucans, and crocodiles.

Andrew had hoped to see sunny beaches along Mexico's coast. But it was raining. The beaches were gray and dull. But Andrew did see birds called egrets and grackles.

Andrew's bus went through La Paz, Bolivia. The road was more than two miles high! Andrew saw the Uyuni salt flats in Southern Bolivia. They make up the world's largest salt desert.

PARAG

URUGUAY

BOLIVIA

ARGENTINA

CHILE

PACIFIC OCEAN

Andrew crossed the Equator in Ecuador. He walked along the line between North and South. He had one foot in each hemisphere.

Andrew crossed the border from Ecuador to Peru. The land changed from a jungle to a desert. Here the desert meets the ocean to the west. It meets the mountains to the east.

The final bus ride went through Argentina. Andrew traveled more than 3100 miles. He went to Cordoba. Then he went onward to Ushuaia in Tierra del Fuego. The Strait of Magellan was rough. That made the short ferry ride scary.

Antarctica at Last

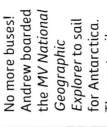

No more buses! Andrew boarded the *MV National Geographic Explorer* to sail for Antarctica. They set sail for Antarctica. Andrew saw a pod of fin whales in front of the ship. He also saw his first iceberg.

ANTARCTICA

ATLANTIC OCEAN

ARGENTINA

CHILE

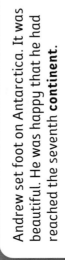

Andrew set foot on Antarctica. It was beautiful. He was happy that he had reached the seventh **continent.**

Andrew visited Deception Island. The whole island is the mouth of a volcano. Andrew went for a swim but he didn't stay in long. The water was 36°F (2°C)!

Andrew took this picture of an all-black penguin on South Georgia Island. Its coloring is rare. This happens when the body has extra melanin. This makes skin, fur, or feathers dark.

Visitors to Antarctica are not allowed to touch wildlife. They must stay 15 feet away from the animals. But a baby penguin jumped into Andrew's lap. Then another one came. It was hard to obey the rules!

Andrew traveled through 14 countries. He covered 10,000 miles in 10 weeks! His trip began on a bus in Washington, DC. It ended on the continent of Antarctica.

Like Amundsen, Scott, and Shackleton, Andrew set a goal. There were bumps along the way, but he pressed onward. It's what explorers do.

Check In What did you find most interesting about Andrew's trip?

Discuss | Compare and Contrast

1. What do you think connects the three pieces that you read in this book? What makes you think that?

2. Compare and contrast the reasons why Amundsen, Scott, Shackleton, and Evans went to Antarctica. How were their reasons alike and different?

3. Andrew Evans uses modern tools, such as a GPS device and a cell phone. How might modern tools have changed the other explorers' expeditions?

4. Choose a haiku. Then find a passage or a photo in another piece that explains or shows what the haiku is describing. Tell how they are connected.

5. What questions do you still wonder about Antarctica or its explorers?